Models of
Liturgical Theology

by James Empereur
Jesuit School of Theology, Berkeley, U.S.A.

This volume of the Alcuin/GROW Liturgical Study is respectfully dedicated to the Reverend Paul Ryan, who for many years has been a model liturgist for Australia.

THE COVER PICTURE

'Windows on Liturgy', based on an idea of the author—see page 9.

First Impression December 1987
ISSN 0951–2667
ISBN 1 85174 057 0

 GROVE BOOKS LIMITED
Bramcote   Nottingham   NG9 3DS

THE ALCUIN CLUB and
GROUP FOR RENEWAL OF WORSHIP (GROW)

The Alcuin Club exists to promote the study of Christian liturgy in general and in particular the liturgies of the Anglican Communion. Since its foundation in 1897 it has published over 120 books and pamphlets. Members of the Club pay a single subscription for the year, and, from 1987 onwards, receive four Joint Liturgical Studies, and other publications of the Club, each year. Address for queries: The Vicarage, Windmill Hill, Runcorn, Cheshire.

The Group for Renewal of Worship has been responsible since 1971 for the Grove Booklets on Ministry and Worship (now the Grove Worship Series), and since 1975 for the quarterly scholarly 'Grove Liturgical Studies'. This latter series has been phased into the new Studies. The address is that of Grove Books Limited, publishers of these Studies.

The Joint Liturgical Studies, beginning from March 1987, represent the coming together of the concerns and resources of both earlier groups, and they are planned and edited by a Joint Editorial Board appointed from both groups. The new Studies are published quarterly by Grove Books Limited. At the time of publishing the Joint Editorial Board consists of the following:

> Colin Buchanan (Chairman of GROW)
> Geoffrey Cuming
> John Fenwick
> Donald Gray (Chairman of the Alcuin Club)
> Trevor Lloyd
> Michael Vasey

The Joint titles for 1987 and 1988 are listed at the back of this volume, and previous titles are available from both addresses. The retail price of the new Studies in 1987 and 1988 is £2.50 each.

CONTENTS

1. Liturgy and Theology

LITURGY AS NORM AND SOURCE OF THEOLOGY

Lex orandi, lex credendi, the law for prayer is the law for faith, is an ancient adage which indicates the church's conviction that the liturgy is indisputably one of the sources from which theology can draw the principles which enable it to elaborate a systematic and scientific exposition of the Christian faith. And this is the case because the liturgy has been seen as a privileged witness of the apostolic tradition. This, in turn, means that the liturgy, especially the early liturgy, has a normative value. This normativity is similar to the normative nature of scripture. It is to be employed in basically the same way. The liturgy is normative, because we presume that the first Christian liturgical experiences were in contact with the pristine and hopefully correct experiences and expressions of the Christ-event.

A norm is some guide or rule against which one judges the authenticity of a present experience. If one wishes to know about the character of some religious experience, some devotion, some doctrine, or teaching in terms of the Judaeo-Christian tradition, it must be measured in terms of the Bible. In that sense scripture sits in judgment upon these experiences and understandings. In the same way does the recognized liturgy of a church judge the prayer of that particular community. A norm is indispensable, for, without it, it is not possible to know if one remains in the Christian tradition.

But while a norm is indispensable, it is not absolute or exclusive. Just as the contemporizing of the word of God cannot be reduced to a biblical fundamentalism, so there can be no question of trying to restore some Golden Age of the liturgy, some ideal rituals from the past which are only meant to be endlessly repeated. That would be an exaggerated emphasis on continuity. Liturgy as a norm. as in the case of scripture, must be seen in terms of the tension involved in the mutual continuity and discontinuity of something living.[1] If liturgy is to be a source of theology, it must be understood and explained as a living reality which is both continuous and discontinuous. It cannot be completely discontinuous, since it could be nonsense to speak of liturgy as a norm if the liturgical experience of the church were but a series of unrelated episodes. Yet one must avoid an excessive emphasis on continuity, which would be little more than the repetition of past ritual structures. Otherwise, the tradition would be dead and could not function as a norm at all.

The question of the normativity of the liturgy leads logically to the issue of distinguishing between a legitimate development and growth in the tradition on the one hand, and that which is a distortion on the other. For instance, is the separation of the sacraments of initiation in the West, with confirmation emerging as a separate sacrament, a legitimate development of dogma and worship? Is the Roman eucharistic prayer, which developed in the fourth and fifth centuries

---

[1] See Walter J. Burghardt, S.J., 'Theologian's Challenge to Liturgy', in *Theological Studies* 35: 2 (June 1974); and John W. O'Malley, S.J., 'Reform, Historical Consciousness, and Vatican II's Aggiornamento' in *Theological Studies* 32:4 (December 1971).

and was the sole eucharistic prayer of the medieval church, an example of distortion? It shows the limitations in language and conceptuality of the time of its historical origins. Many other examples could be raised concerning the question of the authentic development of the liturgy, such as the practice of auricular confession, the importance of the institution narrative in the eucharistic prayer, and the present mode of concelebration.

Authors have indicated that continuity is best located on the level of documents and texts, the structures of the human mind, and the work of previous historians, theologians, and liturgiologists. Thus, in our judging of the legitimacy of the developments in the history of liturgy, three criteria especially seem to the demanded: (1) one must look at the origins of these developments, and measure them against the primitive liturgical experiences of the church to the degree that one can be in touch with those experiences; (2) the developments must be studied in their historical contexts to see if non-theological and non-liturgical reasons were the primary motivating factors; and (3) the development must be judged as (a) meaningful, that is responding to immediate and real needs of the worshippers; (b) as having meaning, that is, it must have internal coherence; and (c) as being true, that is, it must fit into a larger context, such as the meaning of Christian Community, worship of a Trinitarian God, and the like.[1]

The difficult task of assessing true liturgical development does not in any way lessen the fact that theology is a reflection on faith, and can only take shape in terms of real faith in real people. Theology cannot have a life of its own. It is dependent upon believing people. That is why theology without the liturgical experience is dead. Liturgy, not theology, is the most basic mode of communication, whereby the saving actions of God are spoken and accomplished for us. The liturgical assembly of the church is one of the primary places where theological reflection is to take place. In that way the law of prayer is the law of belief. Liturgical theology, then, is the systematic study of this norm. Liturgical theology has the two-fold task of studying (1) how the faith experiences of the worshippers come to expression in the symbolic text and actions of ritual and (2) the effect that the liturgy has on faith itself, how the liturgy is sanctification made visible.

CRITERIA FOR A LITURGICAL THEOLOGY

What is liturgical theology? Despite the extensive writing in this area, there is no clearly settled definition of liturgical theology. Some distinguish between a theology of the liturgy and a liturgical theology. In the former, the emphasis would be on the theological articulation arising from a study of the liturgical texts and actions themselves. In the latter case, liturgical theology would refer more to a theological system with its various branches but as informed by the experience of worship and reflection upon that experience. The distinction may be insufficiently clear to be helpful. But, as a branch of theology, liturgical theology should be both systematic and pastoral. It is systematic when it explores the doctrines of the faith which the liturgy articulates, and when it examines these doctrines in relation to their formulations in the other theological branches such as Christology and

---

[1] David Tracey, *Blessed Rage for Order* (Seabury Press, New York, 1975), chapter 4: 'The Search for Adequate Criteria and Modes of Analysis.'

ecclesiology. It is pastoral when it speaks from and to the church at prayer. It cannot be restricted to the inner life of a theological methodology. Its truth must be validated in the experience of worship itself. Liturgical theology will often take one of two emphases: either (1) an explication of the theology contained within the liturgical celebrations themselves, or (2) the application of theological insights to the church at prayer. In the second emphasis reflective theology brings further explanation to what is achieved in the first emphasis. Ideally, liturgical theology will be an integration of both.

The pressing question today, however, is not whether there can be a liturgical theology, but what the criteria are for such a theology. Several liturgical theologies have been put forth, but the easily observable fact is that too often the actual celebrations do not verify what is being asserted on the theoretical level. Theological models claim one thing; the praying community may be doing something else. Peter Fink has put the question clearly:

'the central question for a liturgical theology will not be one of truth, but rather *credibility*, or, from another point of view, *honesty*. Under what conditions is the Church's prayer an honest enactment of what it claims for itself?'[1]

There may be many liturgical theologies which are true, but they may no longer be believable. The test of a theological model of liturgy is not its correctness, but whether the Christian community at prayer can recognize in that model what it is doing, and more than that, whether such a model assists that community in deepening its experience of God itself in worship.

What is paramount in Peter Fink's discussion of liturgical theology is that any such theology must be based on the limitations of the praying church:

'Worship is thus a language, and the church must always question itself if it is using the language honestly. To the extent that the living members of the praying church back by their lives what they say in ritual, to that extent their ritual will be honest and credible.'[2]

There is a variety of faith experiences in any celebrating community. An adequate liturgical theology not only tolerates this, but is nourished by it.

But there is more to liturgical theology than a careful attention to the praying assembly. It must be informed by a scientific study of the way human beings interact symbolically and celebrate by means of ritual. Part of the data on which the liturgical theologian reflects is the result of interdisciplinary studies. Liturgical theologians cannot simply reflect on the so-called 'bare facts' of actual celebrations. Those experiences must necessarily be understood in the language and conceptual framework of the human sciences. For this reason one finds in liturgical studies frequent references to anthropologists such as Victor Turner,

---

[1] 'Toward a Liturgical Theology' in *Worship* 47:10 (December, 1973) p.602. Since Peter Fink's article appeared, several recent books on liturgical theology have in their various approaches partially addressed his concerns. I take note of three: Aidan Kavanagh, *On Liturgical Theology*, (Pueblo Publishing Co., Inc., New York, 1984); David N. Power, *Unsearchable Riches: The Symbolic Nature of Liturgy*, (Pueblo Publishing Co., Inc., New York, 1984); and Geoffrey Wainwright, *Doxology: The Praise of God in Worship, Doctrine, and Life*, (Oxford University Press, New York, 1980). I especially recommend Power's work for its insightful, balanced, and holistic analysis.

[2] *Ibid.*, p 604.

Clifford Geertz, and Mary Douglas, to sociologists such as Francois Houtart and Robert Bellah, and to psychologists such as Freud, Jung, and Erikson. Liturgical theology, as the other theological disciplines, cannot remain in isolation from these other fields whose proper domain includes human symbolic activity and ritual.

Equipped with the data from the praying church and assisted by interdisciplinary studies, liturgical theologians must articulate the experience of worship in specifically theological categories. These theologians will find in the other theological disciplines models of how to accomplish this task. A helpful and significant way of doing theology today is to eschew the deductive method in favour of one which begins with human experience. But since this experience is varied, there seems to be no single specific starting point except experience itself. Thus, many theologians today adopt what is often referred to as the 'models method'. A now classic example of this is Avery Dulles' *Models of the Church.*[1] The models' approach has proven to be effective in fulfilling the three criteria for a liturgical theology: (1) attention to the limitations of the praying church, (2) consideration of the data of the human sciences, and (3) beginning theological reflection with human experience.

THE USE OF MODELS IN THEOLOGY

There are many reasons why the models' approach is so popular in theology today. Probably, the most cogent of these reasons is the pluralism that characterizes theological understanding. No longer do theologians all say the same thing, if they ever did. It would be difficult to arrive at a discursive agreement among theologians on areas which in the past have been considered substantial to the faith. This is not the same thing as saying that they are generally in disagreement or that they are espousing contradictory positions. Usually they are not. But the reality they deal with is rich and diverse and cannot be grasped in any one formulation.

Another reason for the use of models in theology is our present realization that theological affirmations do not provide exact pictures of reality. Rather, they serve to disclose or represent reality. They interpret reality. Theological models are the result of systematic reflection on theological symbols. They are to be taken seriously but certainly not literally. Theologians cannot claim to be providing us with exact pictures of God, Christ, humanity, grace, sin, and the rest.

A third reason for embracing the models' approach is a very pragmatic one. Since we cannot say everything about reality and since it is not helpful to opt for saying nothing at all, we find that the use of models can be a middle position which allows us to say something about God, grace, salvation, and the like. They give us ways of viewing the world. Models are like windows in a house. Reality is what one sees through the windows. But one cannot look out of all the windows at the same time. To get an adequate view of reality, one must wander from window to window and get a composite view. One should not be content to close one's eyes or to close the shutter on all the windows. Nor is it helpful to pick only one window and be content that such provides the only view of the world. That is what the fundamentalist does. By giving us these models, theologians provide

[1] Doubleday, (Garden City, 1974).

us with a set of relations, terms, images, symbols, and metaphors whereby we can place ourselves in a larger world-view, root ourselves in this time in history, and claim an horizon against which we can understand ourselves and the elements of our Christian faith.

Models are not new things. They have been operative in the physical sciences for some time. For scientists they have provided answers for understanding reality which is not immediately accessible to the senses. Atoms and sub-atomic particles are examples of scientific models. They simplify complex reality so that one can work with it, grasp it, and even manipulate it. Models are especially helpful in science, since they are not pictures of entities, but of networks or structures, of relationships dealing with how something works. Physicists speak of reality in terms of waves and/or particles depending upon the context. Models make it possible to expand knowledge by linking them with a theory. This theory may connect with some theory in another field and there may be an expansion of knowledge through this interaction. But because scientists create these models, they consider them to be partial explanations only. They are appropriate up to a point. They must be used in a contemporary fashion with other models so that they are not too literally construed.

Although in general the use of models in theology followed upon the use of models in science, there are some definite differences between theological models and scientific ones. Scientific models have a pragmatic purpose in helping scientists discover new insights in their fields. Theological models are employed for the purpose of explanation, and this in a more comprehensive way.[1] Theology needs models for explanation since the usual support for our theological affirmations is often challenged. We can no longer assume the acceptance of the biblical material, church tradition, or even personal experience as the authorities in our lives of faith. Because of their comprehensive and complementary character, models can add credibility to our theological claims.

For more on the difference between theological and scientific models see pp.104-107 in *Metaphorical Theology*.

Another difference is that theological models will involve feelings and actions much more than scientific ones.[2] Faith without concomitant action and feeling remains dead. It involves emotional commitment. People's attitudes are shaped more by models than by concepts. Because this is the case many thinkers are challenging the traditional ways in which we understand God. For example, the image of God as father has had effect on the emotional lives of the people who

---

[1] Sallie McFague, *Metaphorical Theology: Models of God in Religious Language*, (Fortress Press, Philadelphia, 1982), pp.104-5. This is one of the best summaries of the use of models in theology. I have, therefore, relied heavily on chapter four: 'Models in Theology.' There are numerous possible references in the area of models both in theology and science. I single out here Ian G. Barbour's *Myths, Models, and Paradigms*, (Harper and Row, New York, 1974). For an approach to models from an aesthetic point of view see Aidan Nichols, O.P., *The Art of the God Incarnate: Theology and Symbol from Genesis to the Twentieth Century*, (Paulist Press, New York; 1980), appendix: 'On Models and Metaphors.'
[2] *Metaphorical Theology*, p.107.

pray by means of this image. Because of its emotional power, the model of the paternity of God is being questioned by feminists today.[1]

In Christian theology, models are ways of dealing with the root-metaphor of Christianity. This root-metaphor is the personal relationship between God and ourselves exemplified in Jesus Christ. It is a metaphor because of the bringing together of seeming contradictions: the love of God for us and the loveless ways of the world. In the words of Sallie McFague:

'The content of the root-metaphor of Christianity is a model of personal relationship, exemplified in the parables and with its chief exemplar Jesus himself, a tensive relationship distinguished by trust in God's impossible way of love in contrast to the loveless ways of the world.'[2]

Models are a kind of metaphor because thought and language are inherently metaphorical. We see one thing in terms of another. This is possible because there is tensive character to metaphors in that they assert something about reality by making a judgment of similarity and difference between two thoughts in permanent tension with one another. They re-describe reality in an open-ended way and with an effective power. Thought, images, and ideas are changed or influenced by being brought into relationship with one another without losing their own identity. This means that metaphors have structuring possibilities. The tension must remain. Because metaphors have structuring possibilities, models can develop from them. Metaphors are poetic happenings. Models organize, selectively re-structure, re-interpret our perceptions, and are part of an intellectual tradition. Both give access to the real. Models are a mixture of conceptual and metaphorical language.

Models, then, are dominant metaphors with comprehensive, organizational potential. Theological models are ways of structuring the root-metaphor of Christianity. As dominant metaphors, theological models gather the images of the Christian tradition in differing ways. They assemble the subordinate images and they relativize concepts at the higher level. They organize the network of meaning called Christianity. As with any religious tradition, Christianity is known through its root-metaphor and the subordinate models which support and enrich it.[3]

Jesus Christ is the root-metaphor of Christianity without whom Christianity would not be. The story of Jesus is not the whole of the Christian paradigm but it continues to be the principal way in which the Christian faith is transmitted across generations. The liturgy is but the ritualized way of narrating that story. Jesus Christ not only tells us about the relationship of God to this world, he also demonstrates it in his life. He is the way to it. The Christian life is pre-eminently one of relationship. It is a relationship of trust in God and a relationship of love toward others. The focus of Jesus's life is on persons and the mode of their relations with one another and with God. As in the case of all metaphors there is

---

[1] For one expanded discussion on this topic see *Metaphorical Theology,* chapter five: 'God the Father: Model of Idol?'
[2] *Ibid.,* p.108.
[3] *Ibid.,* p.110.

similarity and dissimilarity. There is some distance between Jesus and his followers. But this tension helps the relationship to remain open-ended and relative.

In summing up the use of models in theology Sallie McFague says:

'The central role of models in theology is to provide grids or screens for interpreting this relationship between the divine and human. Theological models are dominant metaphors with systematic, comprehensive potential for understanding the many facets of this relationship. Metaphors could not do this alone, for the relationship is a network or structure with too many intricate implications . . . concepts could not do this alone, for the relationship is too complex, rich and multivalent for univocal concepts to define; it needs the simplification of complementary metaphors with their expansive detail to intimate this relationship. The attitudinal and behavioural influence of metaphors (which abstract concepts never have) is needed as well in order to express the power of this transforming relationship. Thus metaphorical and conceptual language must participate in interpreting this relationship and we see this process occurring in a unique way in models.'[1]

Within the root-metaphor of the relationship between the divine and the human, for which there can be no single model or even any supermodel, many models will develop, some with more dominant and permanent status than others. Since these models are not to picture reality, but to interpret relationships, different kinds of them will appear in theology, some concrete, others abstract. Friend and mother are concrete as providence and redemption are abstract.[2] Many models are needed to express the complexity of the divine/ human relationship. No models are adequate. And theology must entertain, interpret, and also criticize the various models. No models can be absolutized. Models are to be taken seriously, but they are to be used, not worshipped. There are two safeguards against such absolutizing: (1) keeping theology in the context of prayer, for in prayer one knows the inadequacy of all images; and (2) keeping in mind that the purpose of theology is not to create a thought system which is self-justifying, but is intended to assist people to encounter God and to grasp their way of being in the world.[3]

A theological system is a network of dominant and subsidiary models.[4] If these models are to work, they must be of a similar or complementary type. But models must be able to cope with anomalies or inconsistencies of various kinds.[5] A certain model may not be able to handle something affirmed in Christian faith such as the presence of evil in the world. A plurality of models makes it possible to endure these various challenges to any system of theology. In the end, theology works when it provides a total, well-integrated and aesthetically satisfying system which facilitates the expansion of the root-metaphor. It seems to do this best through the use of models.

---

[1] *Ibid.*, p.125.
[2] *Ibid.*, p.127.
[3] *Ibid.*, p.131.
[4] *Ibid.*, p.106
[5] *Ibid.*, p.140

2. The Models of Liturgical Theology

In the following pages I will describe seven liturgical models.[1] This is not an exhaustive list, but it is comprehensive. Each model will be discussed according to the same format. First, there will be a description of each model including its primary image as well as the supporting images, metaphors, concepts, and practices. Next the kind of spirituality that each model emphasizes will be sketched. The sketches will show what the nature of our relationship with God is according to each model. And finally, some of the limitations of each will be highlighted.

As we move into these seven models, I wish to reiterate the following:

'It is very important to realize that when the liturgy is described in terms of theological models one is talking about it in metaphorical terms. One is using images that have an evocative power. The use of models in liturgical theology is only an attempt to speak of worship analogously in terms of life experiences. Such images and symbols are able to focus human experience in a new way because they so exceed the powers of abstract thought. These models convey a meaning which is apprehended in a non-conceptual way and which have a transformative effect on the horizons of human life.'[2]

The models examined here are: institutional, mystery, sacramental, proclamation, process, therapeutic, and liberation.

A. THE INSTITUTIONAL MODEL[3]

DESCRIPTION

According to this model, liturgy can be most clearly evaluated by its visible structures. If the ritual is done well, the various ministers function appropriately, and the congregation participates fully, then God's grace will be most completely actualized in the church's worship. The primary image of this model is that of the liturgy as a visible rite. This view considers the liturgy primarily in terms of its ritual structure, its differentiation of roles, and its procedure which is governed by rubrical legislation. It stresses that, if liturgy is to be liturgy at all, it must have some kind of visibility, some leadership, and some accepted mode of procedure. Liturgy according to this model is something which is performed by the presiders for the participants. The liturgical celebration resembles a pyramid in which ordinary worshippers find themselves to be the recipients of the ministry of the clergy. There is a clear-cut distinction between the clergy and the faithful in the liturgy itself. The communion rail of former times in many churches was a striking reminder or such separation. There is a concomitant mentality that the liturgy belongs more to the priest or minister than to the congregation.

The basic visible liturgical structure reflects the structure of our relationship with God, the root-metaphor of Christianity. Liturgy is the perceptible means of grace, whereby the worshippers receive the nourishing benefits given to

---

[1] My previous writing on these models can be found in *Worship: Exploring the Sacred* (The Pastoral Press, Washington D.C., 1987), chapters 6-8.
[2] *Worship: Exploring the Sacred*, p.66.
[3] For a fuller discussion of the church as institution see Avery Dulles' *Models of the Church*, chapter 2.

those who belong to the visible church. The purpose of the liturgy is to assist the worshipper to lead a good Christian life, which is directed toward salvation, which is primarily experienced in the after-life. This is an empirical approach to liturgy where a great deal of stress is placed on what is statistically measurable. Baptisms, marriages, communions, and other sacramental ministries are counted. The worshipping assembly is understood more according to the blue-prints of a building than as a symbol of the human body.

One would not characterize this theological model as one of celebration. It defines liturgy more according to institutional criteria. Often liturgy is understood to be identical to what is found in the approved liturgical books. It is a view of liturgy which has been predominant in most churches for centuries. it has strong endorsement in official church documents and is clearly present in *The Constitution on the Sacred Liturgy*. The liturgical rites become in this model norms for Christian identity and orthodoxy. This leads to a view that the liturgy must be unchanging. The primary symbol of the presence of Christ is the matter and form of the sacraments: consecrated elements, water and formula, sins and absolution, and so on. This model tends to stress liturgy more as a thing than as an event. Great value is placed on proper procedure.

The model of liturgy as institution has a strong legalistic dimension. The observance of liturgical legislation is the minimum requirement for the reality of worship to take place. But it is more than that. A perfectly rubrical liturgy is also seen as a desideratum. The very effectiveness of the liturgy is often measured by the proper observance of the requirements of liturgical law. The emphasis on proper procedure often means that the authenticity of the liturgy is judged according to canonical criteria. Questions about the conferral of grace, the presence of Christ, and the worship of God, are answered in terms of what can be judicially verified. Often such criteria take precedence over the experience of the worshippers. Liturgy takes place when the rules are followed. Liturgical planning is itself reduced to following the law.

The institutional model of liturgy tends to be triumphalistic in character. Here triumphalism is not to be equated with the aesthetics. Grand music, colourful vestments, and other use of the arts do not equal triumphalism. It is the poor and dispossessed of this world who most often appreciate the beautiful dimension of Christian worship. They more readily grasp the transcendent in the wonders of creation as these are found in Christian liturgy. Rather, the triumphalistic attitude is manifested in worship when the liturgy is understood to be unchanging. On this view, liturgy is a perfect gift of the church and cannot be touched or improved. The institutional model does not encourage the questioning of the structures of worship, no matter how outmoded they may be. This model claims that the essentials of the liturgy are unchanging because they have been given to us by Christ. It is not often clear what are the unchanging, divinely instituted, aspects of the liturgy, but presumably they would include the seven sacraments and the hierarchical structure of the church. The conclusion is that liturgy must be hierarchical because the church is. Such a view is triumphalistic. Certainly other liturgical models would understand that liturgy has an hierarchical character but they, more than the institutional model, would make room for the fact that liturgy is a human phenomenon and that the concrete forms of worship must spring from a cultural matrix. Much more of the liturgy is open to change than the institutional world will allow.

In sum, we can say that the liturgy as institution is the model to which we have been traditionally accustomed. It has been dominant in the church for centuries and we have been theologically educated in it until the 1950's. Its images emerge from an understanding of the church as the perfect society. The Christological presupposition is that Christ as priest, prophet, and king has given to the church the mission of teaching, sanctifying, and ruling. This mission is entrusted not to the church as a whole, but to the pope, bishops, and priests. Marcellino de C. Azevedo, S.J., describes this ecclesiology in this way.

'The ecclesiological accent is on the organization and dispensation of power, hence on the judicial dimension. This stress shows up on the three planes of doctrine, sacrament, and administration, which are explicitly linked up with their divine origin. The logical result is the exclusive growth in the Church of the clerical and institutional dimension and the relative atrophy of the charismatic element as well as of the significance of the people of God, particularly the laity. Proper membership in the church is defined as acceptance of the same doctrine, communion in the same sacrament, and obedient subjection to the same pastors—all that being visibly verified.'[1]

SPIRITUALITY

What this model contributes to our understanding of liturgical spirituality is that the spiritual aspect of our lives must be experienced humanly, that it must have a visible dimension. Liturgical spirituality, which is the expression of our relationship with God in terms of the worshipping assembly, presumes that one is ritually involved. It cannot be purely invisible. There is no such thing as purely spiritual Christian spirituality. Just as there must be structure and procedure in the liturgy, so one's spiritual life needs to have some order, and cannot be simply one undifferentiated experience after the other. The liturgy provides a supportive atmosphere and there are clearly delineated expectations on the part of the members of the congregation. This can aid the sense of prayer during the liturgy.

LIMITATIONS

The most serious defect of the institutional model of liturgy lies in what is precisely the major limitation of the institutional model of the church, namely, that there is little New Testament evidence for such an approach to worship. What is described in the scriptures is more flexible, pluralistic, and adaptable. The liturgy of the early church was not characterized by its visible rites, but by the whole community engaging in the act of celebration.

It should not be surprising that the institutional model reinforces the clericalization of the liturgy. The dominance of the model is synonymous with the history of the gradual removal of the liturgy from the people. Moreover, fidelity to the rubrics becomes more significant than the quality of celebration. The authorities in the church appear to call more for attendance at the services

---

[1] 'Basic Ecclesial Communities: A Meeting Point of Ecclesiologies' in *Theological Studies* 46:1 (December, 1985) p.606.

than for authentic worship. Needless to say, liturgy will lack a prophetic quality if the preoccupation is with the observance of liturgical regulations. The dominance of this model of the liturgy has been destructive of the liturgical experience on many levels. Liturgy becomes more the fulfilment of one's duty than a sacrifice of praise and thanksgiving. The human priest inhibits the congregation from experiencing Christ as the one who is priest and chief worshipper in the assembly. And the assembly itself, as the primary symbol of Christ worshipping, is replaced by the rite printed in an official book.

The institutional model raises problems for ecumenical work on the liturgical level. Any church in which the institutional model is dominant would be hostile to the practice of intercommunion. This is clear from the present policy of the Roman Catholic Church and even more so of Eastern Orthodoxy. Ecclesial reality is defined by the parameters of the institution of the particular church. Liturgies of the other churches are deficient in content and life. And certainly anything like a charismatic liturgy would be highly suspect from an institutional point of view.

There are serious limitations to a spirituality which lives under the institutional model. Can a spirituality which structures salvation in terms of those who sanctify and those who are sanctified, be seen as consonant with the biblical call to holiness? If the liturgical rites are viewed primarily as sources of grace, there is the danger that they will be performed more according to magical rules than authentic human experience. How can the exaltation of liturgical law be consistent with the New Testament assurance that we are freed from such a judicial approach? If what is essential in the liturgy cannot change, implying that one's relationship with God is unchanging on the part of God, then what is the value of prayer and how is one to understand the significance of growth in the spiritual life, except in an accidental way? According to this model, worship is too narrowly defined as the source of grace which enables one to save one's soul and to remain within the church. God's presence in all creation is not clearly delineated. An institutional liturgy is concerned wih counting and consuming things. But can this be the spirituality of a community as such? And finally, this kind of spirituality can too easily become identified with receiving answers from one in authority. Spiritual exercises can be little more than following a method in a lifeless way, in a rote and perfunctory manner, rendering the spiritual content vacuous.

It is easy to be negative about the institutional model of liturgy. It has been the dominant model for so long to the exclusion of the other models, that it deserves to be subjected to criticism and reflection. Also it is questionable whether it should ever be a dominant model. It best serves as a support to the other models, one or other of which might have a more central role at any time. Because it can foster the kind of authoritarianism which treats the worshippers as children, it can have deleterious effects on the liturgy which is a community event by nature.

But there are some significant values to the institutional model of liturgy, and that is why this model must be present in good liturgical celebrations. Liturgy as institution means that our contemporary worship is in continuity with the Christian tradition. Our worship today needs to draw upon the wisdom of the past. Ritual structures often embody and maintain important dimensions of religious life which might not spontaneously emerge from community life. These same structures provide identity for worshippers, adults as well as children.

The very notion of liturgical reform demands the institutional model. So much renewal in the church is initiated and promoted by its leadership, whether as individuals or working as a group. Standing liturgical committees, federations of diocesan liturgical commissions, and even parish planning groups make sense in terms of liturgy as institution. And often when the liturgy is an appropriate learning experience, it is the institutional model that is operative.

B. THE MYSTERY MODEL[1]

DESCRIPTION

According to the mystery model of the liturgy the paschal event, the death and resurrection of Jesus Christ, is not merely recalled or commemorated. This mystery of salvation is actually made present in the sacred rite, and our participation is not simply attendance but a full involvement of presence in that paschal mystery. The central image of the mystery model is the church in the act of memorializing. Liturgy equals anamnesis.

This model of liturgy was developed in reaction to the traditional scholastic understanding of grace, which was described in terms of instrumental efficient causality. One of the major liturgical theologians of the twentieth century, Odo Casel, developed his notion of 'mystery theology' as a way of overcoming the excessively mechanistic and impersonal approach which had characterized much of sacramental theology since the middle ages. His approach received approbation in that many of his ideas have been influential in the liturgical theology of the Second Vatican Council.[2]

When Casel speaks of mystery regarding the liturgy, he means a ritual action in which Christ and his saving actions are present. By participating in the rite, the congregation not only is present to the risen Christ, but it participates in those saving actions because these are made contemporary to the congregation by means of the ritual. What Casel attempted to do, despite a questionable philosophical basis, was to restore a sense of realism to the rite. The liturgy is not simply an instrument communicating a grace of an historical event. But that event is now present in the rite and made available for those who enact the rite.

The liturgy is filled with the mystery and the mystery is a complex reality. It means God as God is, and as God exists in creation. It is Christ, not simply the static presence of Christ, but as he is always engaged in his salvific actions, especially his death, resurrection and ascension. Finally, mystery means the

---

[1] This model is distinct from Dulles' model of mystical communion. Much of this latter model would be subsumed under my model of sacrament.

[2] Odo Casel, *The Mystery of Christian Worship*, ed. Burkhard Neunheuser, O.S.B., (The Newman Press, Westminster, MD, 1962); 'Mysteriengegenwart,' in *Jahrbuch fuer Liturgiewissenshaft*, 8 (1928) 'Le Mystère de la Fête', in *La Maison Dieu*, 1 (1945). Charles Davis, 'Odo Casel and the Theology of Mysteries', in *Worship* 34 (1960); L. M. McMahon, 'Towards a Theology of the Liturgy: Dom Odo Casel and the "Mysterientheorie" ', in *Studia Liturgica* 3 (1964); Berkhard Neunheuser, 'Masters in Israel: Odo Casel' in *Clergy Review* 55 (1970).

same active Christ as he operates in the church and the sacraments. This third sense of mystery is at the heart of Casel's liturgical theology. The mystery of the liturgy is neither an external instrument nor invisible grace. It has a sacramental mode of being. It is described in terms of the reactualization theory of the sacraments. The saving deeds are made present again through the cultic action. It differs from the scholastic view in that it is not just the power of the effect of Christ's saving deeds which are found in the liturgy, but these very deeds themselves are present and active. Somehow the historical events of salvation which constitute the root-metaphor of Christianity are made contemporaneous to the modern day worshipper. They are not completely trans-temporal events that break into this world from the outside, nor are they actions which are in essence heavenly ones, the liturgy being but a weak reflection of them. Yet these historical actions of Christ are not made present again in their historical trappings. It is the mystery content which is made available in today's ritual action.[1]

In the church's act of remembrance Christ is alive and active. Christ *and his saving work* is reactualized through the anamnetic action. Through effective commemoration the church participates in this saving activity. The mere presence of Christ if not enough for an authentic liturgical celebration. The liturgy is not a means for producing the body and blood of Christ. Redemption itself must be present, and this takes place by means of the church's creative imagination, its productive memorializing. We are not simply recipients of the grace of Christ, viewers of his presence produced before us. We participate in his death and resurrection in a mystical way. It is a real, although sacramental, joining with Christ in his salvation of the world. When the church recalls this salvation in its liturgy, that redemption itself is present. Casel's insight was to move the liturgical reality away from an impersonal causality to a community action of remembrance.

The mystery model, especially as articulated by Casel, although in many ways embraced by theologians of the Second Vatican Council, has been consistently criticized. How the past mysteries of Christ can be rendered present today was never satisfactorily explained by Odo Casel. Although on the level of theological insight he transcended the mechanistic approach to grace of his time, he did not have the philosophical equipment which would have enabled him to give his position a less challengeable foundation.[2] Nevertheless, his basic understanding of how the liturgical assembly memorializes has received support from two areas of study today. First, a better understanding of the Jewish notion of recall ('*zikkaron*' or '*anamnesis*')[3], especially as this has been elaborated in biblical research, and

---

[1] For a sympathetic discussion of Casel's reactualization theory see Louis Bouyer, *Liturgical Piety*, (University of Notre Dame Press, 1955), chapters 7ff.

[2] For a brief critique of Casel's theory see Cyprian Vaggini, OSB, *Theological Dimensions of the Liturgy*, (The Liturgical Press, Collegeville, 1976), 104ff.

[3] A brief explanation of the concept of anamnesis can be found in the *Theological Dictionary* of Karl Rahner and Herbert Vorgrimler (Herder and Herder, New York, 1965). Part of this description includes: 'Thus anamnesis may be theologically defined as the ceremonial representation of a salutary event of the past, in order that the event may lay hold of the situation of the celebrant. Unlike many liturgical acts in other religions, Judaeo-Christian anamnesis presupposes that, although the event has and retains its historical uniqueness, it is at the same time present, that is, remains in force as an accomplished fact.' See also 'Anamnesis' by Allan Bouley, OSB in Joseph A. Komenchak, Mary Collins, and Dermot Lane (eds.) *The New Dictionary of Theology* (Michael Glazier Inc., Wilmington, 1987).

second, the studies on the eucharistic prayer, lend considerable credence to the mystery theology of Casel.

The biblical notion of *zikkaron* is found in Deuteronomy 6.1-19, where it refers to the recalling and actualizing of the saving events of the Exodus and covenant. This anamnesis of the Exodus and the desert period is the subject matter of chapter eight of Deuteronomy. But Casel did not pay sufficient attention to the biblical understanding of effective commemoration which would have supplied a more adequate basis to his own theory.

The result of research in the meaning and structure of the eucharistic prayer is too vast and complicated to be rehearsed here.[1] But these studies in general are consistent with the biblical research in the area of Jewish memorializing. Although many writers on the theology and practice of the eucharistic prayers do not employ Casel's 'mystery-theology' categories, they follow his fundamental insight. And the important point is that this model of the liturgy which takes its name from Casel is not confined to Casel's system. It is rather that he had an insight which identified a model of liturgy which has been and is still operative in our liturgical celebrations.

In the mystery model, the presence of Christ is understood in a cosmic way. It is not a presence which is limited to the sacraments. Christ is truly present in the word of God, in the liturgical year, and in other actions of the church as in the eucharist. The presence of Christ is one and cannot be divided up. This is true because Christ's saving action is one. Christ is not divisible. It makes sense in this model to speak of the reality of Christ's presence in blessings and in preaching. How this takes place is itself a mystery and is understood with the eyes of faith.

In the mystery model of liturgy, salvation becomes visible. It is visible because the sacramental mode is visible. Through symbolic activity the content of the cultic mystery is set forth. The saving works of Christ are rendered incarnationally through the sacramental reality. But the sacramental way of being is not the same as the natural or the historical. The liturgy itself exists in time, but the content does not. That is, the mystery is not held to any point in time. If that were the case, then there would be a repetition of Christ's saving actions which is theologically unacceptable. In that sense Christ's actions are eternal or trans-historical. The action of Christ is one without a before or after.

There is but one mystery, but it is manifested in many events. The chief events are the death, resurrection, and ascension. What is rendered present is the

---

[1] There are numerous studies on the eucharistic prayer. I list here a few that might be the source for further research. Enrico Mazza, *The Eucharistic Prayers of the Roman Rite,* (Pueblo Publishing Company, New York, 1986); Raymond Moloney, S.J. *Our eucharistic Prayers in Worship, Preaching and Study,* (Michael Glazier, Inc., Wilmington, DE, 1985); John Barry Ryan, *The Eucharistic Prayer: A Study in Contemporary Liturgy* (Paulist Press, New York, 1974); Frank Senn (ed.), *New Eucharistic Prayer: An Ecumenical Study of Their Development and Structures* (Paulist Press, New York, 1987). Also Grove Liturgical Studies, e.g.: 8–*Hippolytus: A Text for Students with Translation, Notes and Commentary* by Geoffrey Cuming; 20–*The Development of the New Eucharistic Prayers of the Church of England* by Colin Buchanan; 24–*Addai and Mari—The Anaphora of the Apostles: A Text for Students* edited by Bryan Spinks; 28—*He Gave Thanks: An Introduction to the Eucharistic Prayer* by Geoffrey Cuming.

paschal mystery, the *transitus Christi*. The Christian Pasch is the central mystery and so Easter is the paradigmatic feast in this model. The liturgical year is a symbolic elaboration of Easter. The full mystery is present in each celebration but it cannot be exhaustively grasped in one act. It, therefore, needs the space of the liturgical year so that it can be experienced as the pattern of the church's spirituality.

SPIRITUALITY

A liturgical spirituality from the mystery perspective would be focussed on the Christ-event. To be in relationship with God would mean experientially rendering the mystery of God present in one's life. To be a spiritual person would involve directing one's life toward participating in the redeeming work of Christ. To be a Christian would mean belonging to a community which remembers so effectively that what it memorializes is reactualized. It is a spirituality which recognizes and celebrates Christ's working in the world in ways which are not strictly sacramental. While what Christians do is performed in time, their spirituality is really a participation in a trans-historical reality. For mystery model Christians the past, present, and future converge in their experience of God.

A mystery model spirituality is synonymous with taking on the personhood of Christ. To meditate on the Jesus of the gospels is not a nostalgia-trip but an attempt to reactualize the reality of Christ, not just as a present reality, but as that which actually saves. This is a distinctly Easter spirituality. The spiritual life itself will be imaged as a kind of passage modelled after Christ's own great passage of death and resurrection. Probably in no other model is Easter and the resurrected Christ so prominent as in this one.

And probably in no other model is the liturgical year taken so seriously. Some have suggested that if you take Casel to his logical conclusions, one would have to maintain that one actually ascends with Christ on the feast of the Ascension, participates in the kingship of Christ on the feast of Christ the King and the like. That may be letting go of the tensive character of the root-metaphor of Christianity and moving in the direction of literalism. More helpful, and more in accord with the mystery model at its best, is to see the church year as a symbol. It is to move away from the historicization which has so rendered our understanding of liturgical time dysfunctional.[1]

The church year is not the biography of Jesus Christ. Holy week is not the walk-through of Christ's final week on earth. The major feasts are not times when we engage in some kind of pretence that we are following the life of the Jesus of the Gospels. This historicization takes place when we begin the church year with Advent as a preparation for the coming of the infant Saviour, when Lent becomes a period of preparation for the passion, death and resurrection, when the Easter triduum is split into three distinct feasts, and when Easter, Ascension, and Pentecost are understood as telling us something historical about the post-resurrection Jesus.

Rather the church year is a symbolic pattern of our spirituality. We image our encounter with Christ, we experience our relationship with him through the symbolic character of liturgical time. Symbols are such that they can be engaged

---

[1] *Worship: Exploring the Sacred,* chapter 13.

on differing levels and in many ways. Through the course of the year we can celebrate our life in Christ as promised (Lenten period), as fulfilled (Easter triduum and Easter season), as lived out (ordinary time), and as future life in Christ promised (Advent, Christmas, Epiphany).[1] In the mystery model we can find the church year not as an attempt to write the history of Jesus, but as a form of the church's spirituality. It is a way of dealing with the root-metaphor of Christianity by reactualizing our life in Christ according to the pattern by which the church celebrates in an anamnetic way.

LIMITATIONS
Despite its realistic emphasis spirituality, according to the mystery model, could well confirm an other-worldly perspective in which there is no bridge between the Paschal Christ and the daily deaths and resurrection of ordinary life. Thus the danger of this kind of spirituality is that it becomes an end in itself. The church exists for liturgy rather than liturgy being in the service of the church. This is a common criticism of Eastern Orthodoxy whose liturgical life is strongly characterized as being in the mystery model. Spirituality and liturgy become a world within the world, an escapists' enclave.

The greatest danger of an over-emphasis on this model is its irrelevance to the church's mission. This problem has been well summed up by Azevedo, who stresses that the mystery of the church is intimately bound up with the mystery of Jesus Christ, and no less with the understanding of his mission. Liturgical theology cannot avoid the fact that the proclamation of the kingdom is intrinsically connected with its realization. He points to three levels on which the mystery of salvation must be realized and, therefore, recognized and celebrated in the liturgy.

'The first level is the redeeming and saving liberation from sin that marks the human race as a whole and the individual person. The second level has to do with sin in terms of its interpersonal and social projections, insofar as it expresses the perversion of God's plan as manifested in the concrete human organization of social, economic, and political realities that have been created by human beings and that affect humanity. The third level has to do with liberation from sin as the latter is incorporated into the gestation of culture and history over centuries, which in turn is often the wellspring of sin on the two other levels and vice versa. These three levels of salvation, redemption, and liberation are a replica of God's activity with the people of Israel, hence of the history of our salvation as designed by God.'[2]

C. THE SACRAMENTAL MODEL
DESCRIPTION
According to this model the church is Christ's body and the liturgy can be seen as the fullest expression of what it means to be church. It is an outward symbol of a present spiritual reality. This reality, God's life, seeks visibility, and finds itself

---

[1] *Ibid.*, p.204.
[2] Azevedo, 'Basic Ecclesial Communities,' p.619.

really present in the gathered worshipping assembly. In this model, liturgy means the worshipping, grace filled community.

The sacramental model of liturgical theology is widely used. It is probably the most prominent model in the *Constitution on the Sacred Liturgy*. It is acceptable to Eastern, Roman, and Protestant Christians. This model has a strong ecclesiological base in that it presupposes the view that the church is the primordial sacrament.[1] Liturgy is the expression of the church and for the building up of the church. Vatican II is emphasizing this model when it says: 'The church is a kind of sacrament of intimate union with God and of unity with all mankind; that is she is a sign and instrument of such union and clarity'[2] and 'the liturgy is the summit toward which the activity of the church is directed; at the same time it is the fountain from which all her power flows.'[3] The ecclesiology which forms and permeates this model of the liturgy has been summed up by Azevedo:

'. . . Christ is a sacrament and so is the Church. Christ is the sign and visible presence of the invisible God, the efficacious power of salvation for the indiviudal and the whole people of God. As institution and communion, the Church is sign and visible presence of Christ: accepted by faith and lived both really and mystically by the ecclesial community in the unity of the same faith. Indeed, the Church is even more sacrament than sign. Through its visible actions the church not only signifies but dynamically produces and makes visible the reality of salvation that it represents and announces. The church, then, is a grace-happening, and not just in the sense that it effects and administers the sacraments. It is a grace-happening as well because in the life of believers, who are the church, we see operating and unfolding faith, hope, love, freedom, justice, peace, reconciliation, and everything else that establishes human intercommunion and humanity's communion with God.'[4]

It would be a mistake to see the sacramental model of the liturgy as the one that stresses the individual sacraments of the church. That may be more characteristic of the institutional and mystery models. Rather, this model flows from an understanding of the human person as an incarnate reality. The very structure of human life is symbolic. The body is the symbol of the human spirit. The corporeal and the spiritual are inextricably linked. One flows through the other. This model is probably the most incarnational of all. Thus, the liturgy is seen primarily as the incarnate reality of church. It is a sacrament of the sacrament of the church. The sacramental emphasis is on the community as such rather than on the specific sacramental symbols themselves.

---

[1] The major works in the last quarter century on the sacramentality of the church include: Otto Semmelroth, *Church and Sacrament* (Fides Publisher, 1965); Edward Schille-beeckx, *Christ, the Sacrament of the Encounter with God* (Sheed and Ward, 1963); Karl Rahner, *The Church and the Sacraments*, (Crossroad, New York, 1963); and, of course, Dulles' *Models of the Church*.
[2] Vatican II, *Lumen Gentium*, November 21, 1964, art. 1.
[3] Vatican II, *Sacrosanctum Concilium*, 4, December, 1963, art. 10.
[4] Azevedo, 'Basic Ecclesial Communities', p.608.

Within the parameters of this model the sacraments of the church would be considered as social symbols which are dialogic in character. We do not baptize ourselves; we do not anoint ourselves; we do not celebrate the eucharist alone. As communal symbols sacraments call for participation. Through this participation the church as sacrament is created and the liturgy is the expression of it.

The images of Body of Christ and People of God associated with the model show how central is the notion of church as community. Unlike the institutional model, however, the focus is not on the visible structures of the liturgical assembly. Rather it is the community formed by the union of grace which is prominent here. It is this grace-filled union which makes of the assembly a Christian community, one which is more than a purely sociological phenomenon. Authentic worship is not judged according to juridical terms but the degree of union which is deeper than any human union. The purpose of the liturgy is to constitute and express the lasting union between God and Christians. What is articulated in the liturgy is grace as a communal gift.

There are practical ramifications when one sees the liturgy in terms of these two images of Body of Christ and People of God. Among the liturgical implications of the Body of Christ image would be (1) diversity of roles and a proper ordering of roles within the liturgy, and (2) unity and diversity within the liturgy. A body grows, develops, and renews itself continually, but often slowly. Still today congregational participation advances with measured pace. While there are now a variety of ministries available such as that of lectors, musicians, ushers, and eucharistic ministers, it takes time to find qualified ones. The leaders of worship do not change their style overnight. Our concern should be that there is movement. But, to be deep and lasting change, it may need to be slow.[1]

The image of Body of Christ rejects the notion of uniformity in the liturgy. In fact it promotes diversity. The human organism is quite adaptable. The ritual should be flexible enough to admit of extensive adaptation. It cannot be a question of unity or diversity, but of unity in the midst of diversity. There can be no common denominator liturgy, and yet there must be enough balance among the various types of liturgies so that the richness of diversity is not lost to a kind of narrow sectarianism.[2]

The image of the people of God has a number of liturgical implications. There must be continuity with the past if this people is to have any identity and there must be renewal if the tradition is to continue to thrive. Fred Krause, O.F.M., cap., observes:

'in the immediate aftermath of Vatican II there was a tendency to see continuity with the past and adaptation to new conditions as opposites. To favour continuity was judged conservative; to favour adaptation was labelled as liberal. Such a dichotomy was unfortunate. If the church is a

---

[1] Fred Krause, O.F.M. cap., *Liturgy in Parish Life,* (Alba House, New York, 1979), p.57. He discusses the practical implications of the community oriented images of the liturgy.

[2] *Ibid.,* pp.55-58.

people, then both continuity and adaptation are inseparable elements of her living tradition. Continuity and adaptation are often in tension, but that tension should be a creative one that leads to growth and vitality, not divisiveness and destruction.'[1]

This image also implies sensitivity to any individual community's past history when trying to build up a sense of unity which should be helpful to worship. And since liturgy presupposes a continuing community, it is important to identify and foster the people's actual experience of fellowship so that there is a communal basis both for the celebrations and the implementation. Invoking the words, 'people of God' will not produce community instantaneously.

The sacramental model brings together the institutional model and the community-orientated models. Liturgy is incarnational and so it must be visible. It is communal and so must be structured. But it is also more than structure. As the mystery model stresses, there is something really going on and this is grace realizing itself in coming to visibility. The community's spirituality is taking on historical expression. Liturgy celebrates the transformation that is taking place through the power of the spirit which is at the heart of this union of grace.

The sacramental model does not claim a monopoly on the grace of God. Rather as is the case with the individual sacraments, liturgy is a paradigm of how God is working in the world. Salvation is found outside the church and liturgy. But just as the church is the clearest expression of what Christ is about, so the liturgy is the most articulate form of the Christian community's experience of God. Liturgy removes ambiguity of how grace is present in the world. The liturgy witnesses to what is often obscure, namely, that God is ever present and active in all creation.

The sacramental model then deals with the root-metaphor of Christianity by contextualizing our relationship with God in Christ in terms of the grace-filled community. On the one hand grace which is imperceptible receives structure, and, on the other hand, the visible character of the community itself continues to be shaped by the lives infused with the Holy Spirit. Worship, then, is grace made empirical in a communal way. And sacramentality is more adequately realized in the *Sacramentum Mundi* than in the seven specific actions of the church.

SPIRITUALITY

It would seem that the sacramental model when applied to our common spirituality would be ideal. Its stress on the church as community would safeguard one from any extreme individualism in spirituality. Since the structure of human existence is seen incarnationally, the human personality becomes the meeting place of God and ourselves. Spirituality is a dialogic relationship with God in which the personal and bodily encounter is the locus of this conversation. The direction and purpose of one's spirituality is to make oneself into a sacrament, a revelation of the deeper union that exists between Christians. Such a spirituality would be distinguished by its concern to show forth the dynamism of grace which is found beneath the structure of the church and our personalities.

---

[1] *Ibid.*, p.52. See also Walter Burghardt's 'Theologians' Challenge to Liturgy.'

A sacramental spirituality would be sufficiently humble to realize that its way of dealing with God is not an exclusive one. God is always working in the world and all situations and persons can potentially be the sacraments of the saving power. With this all encompassing incarnational approach, there would be no denigration of the human body, although the emphasis would be more on the symbolic value of the body than on its flesh or carnality. The body is important so that one can lead a life of communal holiness.

Because the sacramental model points to the union with God and with one's neighbour as the essential foundation of the church, it raises up the action of the Holy Spirit. Grace is the integrating element in the Christian community and it is the Holy Spirit which is the source of that life. The Spirit is what makes the liturgy the outward expression of the invisible life of the church. The sacramental liturgy will have a strong epicletic character, that is, the liturgy articulates and celebrates the ways in which the Spirit of God brings about the union of the worshippers.

A sacramental spirituality is basically a lay spirituality. People of God includes all the people. It is the whole church which sums itself up in the liturgy. The church is not represented primarily by the clergy. The ordained ministers take their place within a community which is ever more aware of its role in the world. The sacramental model is reflected in those situations where lay persons serve as ministers of the sick and the eucharist. When they perform specifically liturgical roles of functions which are directed toward worship, or which are for the Christian well.being of individuals and communities, they are clear signs of the church as sacrament. Perhaps, it is for reasons such as these that the catechumenate of the RCIA best represents liturgically, educationally, and spiritually the meaning and significance of the sacramental model.

LIMITATIONS

As should be evident from official documents of the church, this form of liturgical theology can be easily expressed in a highly rhetorical way. Liturgy is spoken of in such an exalted fashion, that the expression becomes incredible. Relating the earthly liturgy to the heavenly liturgy runs the risk of some of the limitations of the mystery model which tends toward artificiality. And often the social and ethical dimensions of the liturgical assembly do not receive their due.

There is a necessary and undeniable tension in this model because its foundational concept is community. Often references to the fact that liturgy presupposes community can cause a great deal of frustration. The ordinary experience of community at liturgy is often highly deficient. The language is ideal; the real situation is disappointing. Where can one find the kind of community spoken of so romatically by liturgists and homilists? The desire for perfect community before one can worship with others can lead to disillusionment and abandonment of liturgical practices.

Obviously then, those whose spirituality can be described according to this model must be circumspect about their understanding of community. On the one hand, an unrealistic idea can emerge as a way of escaping from the dismal actualities of human community or, on the other, a sense of hopelessness can permeate this spirituality because the possibilities of community seem too utopian. Unless this search for human community is tempered with considerable realism, this sacramental type of relating to God will become dysfunctional. The temptation will then be to have the rhetoric substitute for the reality. Liturgy becomes a form of 'religious conversion' or 'spirit-filled sharing' where all that religious language masks over its social and ethical irrelevancy.

One of the major limitations of this model is found when the notion of sacrament is restricted to the specific sacraments of the church. Liturgy becomes equivalent to the rites of the church and informal situations of worship are excluded. And, while sacramental spirituality comes to expression in formal worship, it must still be rooted in all of human experience. Like the mystery model it places the mystery of God at the centre of human life. But it must also challenge the worshipper about the distinction they make between the sacred and the secular. The sacramental model will have failed if our meeting with God in the visible, symbolic activity of the sacraments does not alert us to the presence of God outside of the liturgy in nature, communities, persons and societies.[1]

D. THE PROCLAMATION MODEL[2]

DESCRIPTION

The proclamation model of liturgical theology is one in which the dialogic relationship of God to the world is made evident in the structure and shape of the liturgy. In the words and actions of the liturgy, God proclaims the word, Jesus Christ. We, the church respond to the same word, humanly dwelling with us. That response must be for us a moment of faith and decision. Thus the primary image of the liturgy according to this model is that of Christ and his community proclaiming and responding.

Of all the models, this may be the most ecumenical, for Christian theologians of differing traditions are at home with the liturgy as a proclamatory event. Liturgy, like the church, is constituted in and by the proclamation of the word of God. The sacramental actions of the liturgy are the 'visible words' so often spoken of by Lutheran theologians.[2]

Proclamation is the model of Karl Barth and Rudolf Bultmann. It is also the model of modern Roman Catholic theologies insofar as they grew out of the biblical, liturgical revival. For Barth the church, and so the liturgy, is not a permanent institution. It is called into being by the word of God in scripture. It is this proclaimed word which gives rise to faith. The word of God is the ultimate authority in the church. This word renews the church. The constant proclama-

---

[1] For more about the sacramental model of the church see Dulles, *Models of the Church*.
[2] For an elaboration of this model see *Worship: Exploring the Sacred*, chapter 9. See also Dulles' herald model in *Models of the Church*.
[3] Augustine said: 'the word comes to the element and so there is a sacrament, that is, a sort of visible word' (*In Johannem*, 80, 3). One Lutheran theologian begins with this insight to develop an interpretation of the Christian sacraments. See Robert W. Jenson, *Visible Words*, (Fortress Press, Philadelphia, 1978).

tion of the saving event of Jesus constitutes the mission of the church. Bultmann also sees the word of God as central. For him the church is a creation of the New Testament. Its purpose is to proclaim the word in its worship. The church comes into existence in the kerygmatic event in the proclamation of and response to the word. Both theologians clearly stress the place of the word over church:

> 'These two theologians assume the importance of the community to which the word is addressed. The word is the glue around which the community gathers. The response of faith given to the word by the community is what gives the latter its meaning and reason for being.'[1]

Roman Catholic theologians would tend to stress in addition, or as a corroective, that the word of God, in becoming human, lives on in the church. There he shares his life with us. There his message is announced. For the theologians of the more catholic persuasion, more account would have to be taken of the institutional model than was taken by either Barth or Bultmann. But, like them, Catholic theologians would maintain that the teaching church is not above the word but derives its own starting-point and nourishment from that word. Moreover, it is not enough for the church to hear the word and then proclaim it. It must translate it for contemporary people.

The model is strongly evangelical and kerygmatic. It emphasizes evangelization, announcing the paschal mystery, and calling people to conversion. Of all the models of the liturgy there is none that takes more seriously the priority of God in the process of salvation. God speaks first in the dialogue between God and us. The basic attitude of the worshipper is that of the listener. Through the act of listening, God becomes present and a relationship with God becomes a possibility. This dialogic union with God is created through communication.

This communicative event of liturgy is a human event. The presence of God to us is a human one which takes place in a human way. This human way is the way of language. Also, full human presence must be personal. Personal presence must be adequate to the partners in dialogue. This adequacy is achieved through the event of language. In the case of liturgy the language is Jesus Christ. As the word of God, he is the language of God. Christ does not exhaustively communicate the reality of God. But his communication is adequate enough to make sharing in God's life in terms of mutual, human, personal presence a real possibility.

The language referred to in this model is not any kind of language. It is more than mere verbal communication. It is not simply the providing of information. It is not the language we use to negotiate in our daily living. It is not the language of conversation, the exchange in the supermarket, the language of TV or radio, and the language of the business luncheon. Rather it is the kind of language whereby something 'happens', something is created. A new encounter, a deepening of a relationship, a shock, a surprise, a bonding, with or without words, are the result of this kind of language. This wider sense of language refers to the way

---

[3] Azevedo, 'Basic Ecclesial Communities,' p.612.

that human beings become mutually present in an adequate and often fully human way. This is what is meant by a language-event.[1]

Language-event means that human presence depends upon language. Our personal reality is constituted by human presence brought about by such an event. For instance, we may be physically crowded together in an aeroplane. We share a common experience with a certain group of people for a designated amount of time. There is often eye-contact and other kinds of physical interaction. But little that is specifically human is going on. However, there are times when we meet the persons next to us in a way in which we learn more about them. That is human presence. Perhaps during moments of turbulence, as the plane flies through a storm, the others reveal to us their anxieties and fears and seek comfort and support. This is more than the simple communication of information. It is true proclamation. For at that moment reality is constituted through language. We are in relation to those persons to the degree that they are present to us through this language-event.

Proclamation is an event because it is creative. It brings meaning into our lives. It calls us to decision. We can accept or reject the challenge. Whether we accept or reject, a new relationship to others or things is brought into existence. Such would be the case when terrified people in the plane reach out to us. We must accept or reject. It is impossible to remain neutral in such a situation. And so it is easy to see how this understanding of proclamation is related to community. As I have written elsewhere.

'The eventful word both depends on the community and is constitutive of community. A community is that group of people who share the same language, who assent to the same proclamation in their lives. The community of the church is that group of individuals who have heard the proclamation of the word of God and who now live according to the vision put forth by that language-event. They are people with the Christian vision and the Christian language because what they share is Jesus Christ with a certain explicitness. This is so because Christ is for them their eventful word.'[2]

Liturgy, then, is a language-event in which God and we become mutually present. It is a dialogue in which God proclaims through Jesus Christ through the gospel and the sacraments and in which we respond through Jesus Christ in the language of praise and thanksgiving. Christ is God's best proclamation as he is our most adequate response. He is the fullest proclamation of the community. This model deals with the root-metaphor of Christianity precisely in these terms. The divine-human relationship is manifested in the metaphor of Jesus Christ, who in his present resurrected life is both proclamation and response.

---

[1] For an introduction to the notion of language as event, see Robert W. Funk *Language, Hermeneutic, and Word of God,* (Harper and Row, New York, 1966). See especially chapter 2: 'Language as Event: Bultmann and Heidegger,' and chapter 3: 'Language as Event: Fuchs and Ebeling'.

[2] *Worship: Exploring the Sacred,* p.78.

Christian liturgy, as the place where the paschal mystery is permanently proclaimed in the dialogue between God and the worshippers, is the most explicit expression of the Christian life and the most articulate experience of what it means to be church. In the liturgy, the church is both expressed and constituted through proclamation, because the four elements of liturgy: assembly, word, leadership, and meal point to the four elements of church: community, biblical tradition, ministry, and sharing.

Perhaps, more than any other model, the one of proclamation has definite concrete implications for ritual structure and liturgical planning. The theological rhythm of proclamation and response is reflected in the ritual action. It too must be one of proclamation and response. The essential movement of a liturgical rite is one where there are moments of intensification followed by moments of greater receptivity. On the largest scale we see this in the traditional structure of liturgy of word and action, the former being the proclamation and the latter the response. This is clearly seen in the movement of word to eucharist, word to baptism, word to reconciliation, and so forth. But even within these larger components of the liturgy, one can analyze the rite according to the proclamation/response rhythm, as for instance, reading=proclamation, psalm=response, or eucharistic preface=proclamation and *Holy, Holy, Holy Lord*=response. Successful liturgical celebrations depend upon a sensitivity to this rhythm.[1]

SPIRITUALITY

A liturgical spirituality characterized by the proclamation model would have many similarities to that of the sacramental model because both are dialogic in character. But it would be more a spirituality of listening, since it is God who initiates the proclamation in one's life. God speaks first not only in the liturgy but in all the moments of proclamation in ordinary human existence. Those who see themselves in terms of this model tend to be sensitive to the various ways in which God and they themselves are mutually present to each other. All forms of adequate human presence and mutuality are but moments in the continuing dialogue with God. Perhaps, these Christians more than others have a special reverence for the scripture and allow the biblical texts outside of a liturgical setting to function normatively for them in their movement toward God.[2]

A spirituality of proclamation would see more in words than mere verbalization, more in affective touch and sexual expression than certain biological actions, more in every smile and sound of laughter than human spontaneous reaction. Each becomes part of the language whereby they can speak of the experience of God, the language that actually creates this relationship with God. Great concern would be placed on the moment of decision and the spiritual dimension of each call to accept or reject would be identified with greater clarity than usual.

Proclamatory spirituality would also have the stress on community of the sacramental type, but community would be seen as an event of shared language. Christians of the proclamatory type would live their individual lives out of this

[1] For more on this see pp.130-132 of *Worship: Exploring the Sacred*.
[2] See my chapter, 'Liturgical Spirituality', in Malcolm C. Burson (ed.) *Worship Points the Way*, (Seabury Press, New York, 1981) for a discussion of the contrast between institutional and proclamatory spiritualities.

community of shared visions and explicitness. There would be a rhythm of proclamation/response in the daily lives of these people. The spiritual life would not be one-dimensional, but would be characterized by movement from intensification to receptivity back to intensification.

We find this model of spirituality emerging in a special way in those parts of the world where the basic ecclesial communities are prevalent. Since they do not always have access to the sacrament, they depend a great deal on the word. Scripture functions as a catalyst in these communities. What they have to offer to the rest of the church is that scripture must be prayed and reflected upon in immediate relationship with life.

'If it is true for BECs that the Bible is the word of God, it is no less true that God also speaks to us in the language of real life. Bible and life shed light on each other for those who look to them for meaning in faith. The faith and spirituality of BECs are grounded on this foundation.'[1]

LIMITATIONS
One of the deficiencies of this model is that, when emphasized as the way of spiritual growth, there can be a tendency to fundamentalism. As as result of the great reverence for the word, the Bible can become an absolute. Because of their sensitivity to the proclamations of God in human living, proclamatory types might tend to see God giving minute directions concerning the house-keeping details of their lives. Often this is due to an inflated Christology or pneumatology in their prayer lives. Such a Jesus-and-me spirituality can be very individualistic, and such literalism can degenerate into trying to possess the Holy Spirit as one's personal guru. In the liturgy, when the proclamation model takes over, the dialogue ceases and the action is all one way. It is not that the liturgy provides the sure foundation for one's salvation à la the institutional model. Rather, it becomes the place where the congregation can be unconsciously manipulated by the presider or *vice versa*.

Another weakness of the model is that it tends to de-emphasize the institutional or visible aspect of the liturgy. The liturgy becomes primarily the place of personal witness and there is a lack of depth in understanding of how the word of God operates in any culture. It is not enough to proclaim the scriptures in the liturgy. That proclamation must also be inculturated. There must be a way in which the proclamation will be continuous, live on, and be connected with the world and its problems. The danger is that what this model does so well, namely, make judgments on individual lives and societal structures, may never be translated into concrete action, but remain on the level of eschatological witness.

E. THE PROCESS MODEL
DESCRIPTION
Liturgy is an event always in process. The God whom the liturgy celebrates is a changing God who interacts with the world as being both its creator and being

---

[1] Azevedo 'Basic Ecclesial Communities', p.613.

created by it. The worshipping community and the Christ of the liturgy are constantly evolving. Through the liturgy the worshippers appropriate the past, relate to the present, and respond to the allurement of the future. If there is an image of the liturgy in the process model, it would be the world at worship.

The process model of liturgical theology is a response to one of the major theological movements of contemporary times.[1] Process thought is a systematic conceptuality for understanding God and the Christian message, which is rooted in the philosophical position of Alfred North Whitehead. It is a position which stresses the relationship of God to the world as one of union rather than separation. God is intrinsically present and at work in the world. God is inseparable from this world as this world is inseparable from God. The world is the symbol of God and is sometimes referred to as God's body. The world we have is the one of God's activity and existence. The God apart from this world is a meaningless consideration in process thought. Accordingly, there is no room for a view of liturgy which would see it as worship of God beyond this world. Liturgy does not refer us to an absent or utterly transcendent God, but rather reveals to us the God who is working in and through the world toward greater union.

Three key concepts of process thought are also central to a process liturgical theology. They are that reality is highly relational, becoming rather than being is the inclusive category of existence, and reality advances through moments of creativity and novelty. This means in the first place that liturgy celebrates a world of interdependence and interrelatedness. It cannot establish clear-cut parameters around itself and the church as does the institutional model. The lines between church and world and Christ and humanity are blurred. The liturgy brings to expression a whole network of relationships which are coloured by the Christian traditions. Some central foci in this network are clearly Christian but, as one moves from these foci, Christianity becomes less explicit. The liturgy takes into consideration the fact that more is celebrated in the rites than what can be clearly affirmed by Christian theology.

It is process rather than substance which defines the reality of worship. Just as God who is worshipped in liturgy changes and is still considered perfect, so the authenticity of Christian liturgy does not mean that it can be reduced to some unchanging elements. This is not to be seen as a form of religious anarchy. It is rather the affirmation that there is the possibility of growth in even the most

---

[1] For an understanding of process thought one would have to become acquainted with the seminal work of such men as Alfred North Whitehead, Charles Hartshorne, and Teilhard de Chardin. For those seeking an introduction to process theology, I recommend: John B. Cobb Jr., and David Ray Griffin, *Process Theology: An Introductory Exposition*, (Westminster Press, Philadelphia, 1976); Eugene H. Peters, *The Creative Advance*, (The Bethany Press, St. Louis, 1966); Marjorie Hewitt Suchocki, *God, Christ, Church: A Practical Guide to Process Theology*, (Crossroad, New York, 1982). Works on process thought which would be helpful to the area of liturgy would include: Harry Janes Cargas and Bernard Lee (eds.) *Religious Experience and Process Theology*, (Paulist Press, New York, 1976) and Bernard Lee, *The Becoming of the Church*, (Paulist Press, New York, 1974).

basic aspects of life. Furthermore, liturgy is not a finished product. It is an event on the way. The church is not immutable and neither is its liturgy. Both are part of the flow of reality. But the church and liturgy reveal the nature of the direction of the total process. They may point the way in which the stream is flowing, but they are in no way separated from the stream. The liturgy does not flow aimlessly in this stream but advances through the constant experience of novelty and creativity. The world, and so the liturgy, is under the direction of God who constantly brings about the new and so makes possible this movement through the creative advance.[1] Creative advance well expresses how this model re-images the root-metaphor of Christianity.

Although the liturgy may use the language, images, and symbols that presuppose a more classical understanding of God, the God of the process model is one who is personally concerned with the worshippers' problems and desires. This is not the God who has no real relation to the world, who is beyond time and space, who is without feeling and change. Rather the God of Christian worship is affected by what takes place in the liturgy. God is enriched by the prayers and praise of the Christian assembly. This God is also diminished when the quality of liturgy is poor and the congregation does not support by their lives the claims that are made by the ritual. God can see the direction in which the world should best go and God can try to lure the world to greater humanization, but God cannot coerce. Although the world is under the direction of God, it can affect God for better or worse. The liturgy reflects and clarifies how God is part of the fabric of this world.

Process thought attempts to respond to the values of contemporary society which sees change in positive terms. Growth and development are not understood as limitations of perfection, but a form of perfection itself. This is especially true of the image of God in worship. Traditional theology has repeatedly emphasized the immutability of God. But the prayer and songs of the liturgy presume that God is affected by what we do. The process model better than others helps us to see the liturgy as the clearest ritual expression of how God is affecting the world and how the world is contributing to God. This may be expressed as follows:

'God does not enter our world through the liturgy and when we are at worship we are not addressing someone who is outside of the liturgical assembly. God is always there and, because of our ritualizing, God rises to visibility for the community which is gathered together, hears the gospel, shows forth its ministry and shares in the supper of the Lord.'[2]

The liturgical experience of the church is open-ended and always evolving, because the Christ of the liturgy is. He is always in the process of becoming, moving in the direction set forth by God. This does not mean that Christ could become a 'non-Christ.' That would be to misunderstand process thought. There

---

[1] For how some of these concepts are applied to the sacraments see Bernard Lee, *The Becoming of the Church*; Marjorie Hewitt Suchocki, *God, Christ, Church*; and Robert B. Mellert, *What is Process Theology?* (Paulist Press, New York, 1975).

[2] *Worship: Exploring the Sacred*, p.81.

certainly is continuity in the life of Christ and with his death and resurrection. There is always something of the past in the Christ who is the chief worshipper in our liturgy. The point is that there is continuity and not mere repetition. There is always something novel in the advancing liturgical event. The direction of the liturgy is more to the future than to the past. The Christ-event does not remain frozen in history as in the case of the institutional model, nor is it merely re-actualized as the mystery model claims. There is growth and movement in the mystery of salvation each time it is celebrated. For this reason it is necessary to build change into the very structure of worship itself. As Christ is not merely repeated, so the ritual cannot merely repeat what Christians have done before.

In the process model of liturgy the past historical events of Christ are prehended in the experience of the present worshipping assembly. The liturgy advances the growth of the church by incorporating into it that which is new in its contemporary relationships. God, Christ, the church, and the liturgy are all part of this process of becoming, and, in this sense, our liturgical lives are lived from the future. Through Jesus Christ, God is persuading the church in the direction of greater union with Godself. Through the church and the liturgy, Jesus Christ is luring the world in the direction of greater humanization.[1] Liturgy is that special moment in the life of the church where Christian relationality, becoming, and novelty are highlighted and established in a deeper and more unambiguous way. The liturgy is the way the church is maintained in its process of constant creation. Thus, 'the liturgy becomes a celebration of salvation by appropriating the past, by relating to the present and by reponding to the allurement of the future.'[2]

SPIRITUALITY

A process-orientated spirituality would clearly seek the relationship with God in terms of this world. The stress would be on discovering one's spirituality in the experience of one's unity with this universe and the humanity of which one is a participant. This world is the arena of God's working in our lives. One of the chief characteristics of a process spirituality is its highly relational way of being in the world. Such a spirituality would not be sympathetic to making clear-cut distinctions, much less hostile dichotomies, between the sacred and the profane, the spiritual and the material, church and society, Christ and the rest of humanity. Such relationships are more blurred and less easy to delineate.

A process-orientated spirituality would see the striving for perfection as something which has no end-point. There is no question of arriving at the finished product. Nor would one be able to isolate certain immutable constants in such a spirituality. Not that everything changes in an anarchic way, but that it is the directionality of one's total spiritual life which gives identity, rather than any individual component of such a relationship with God.

---

[1] See Norman Pittenger, *The Lure of Divine Love: Human Experience and Christian Faith in a Process Perspective*, (The Pilgrim Press, New York, 1979), chapter 12.
[2] *Worship: Exploring the Sacred*, p.82.

Process spirituality better than most articulates the God of our lives as a God who is very much involved in our living. God is personally involved in our spiritual growth and is deeply interested in how we respond to the call that God makes in our lives. One way of speaking about spirituality according to the process mode is to understand it as the process of making a constant contribution to God. It follows that such a spirituality is open to the creative moments of human living. Novelty is not seen as that which distracts us from personal growth toward God. Rather it is the newness that enters into our lives that is a sign that God is taking the initiative to bring us to Godself.

Process spirituality does not allow for a separation between the body and the mind. We experience our world primarily through our bodies and our bodily behaviour.[1] The direction of a process spirituality is to engage in the process of re-integration at levels of increasing complexity which is to result in a kind of self-consciousness whereby the person transcends nature and themselves.[2] There is never a resolution between the tension of good and evil in our lives. Perfection means 'the best possible' for any individual. There is no abstract perfection which has no real relevance to the concrete world of events. Actual perfection has reference to the actual state of affairs. Perfection involves limitation, relevance, and community.

To sum up the meaning of the process spirituality an example may help. If we truly affect God, then when we become more fully human, that is, whenever we enrich our own lives, we make a contribution to God. We have enriched our world through our living and God becomes more fully God to the degree that this world contributes to this process. Thus, if I am praying for my sick friend, I hopefully become a better human being. I am making a contribution to God which I would not be doing had I not prayed. God is continually entering into the lives of us humans. And once God has been enriched by my humanization process, God enters into the life of my friend in a way that God would not be able to do if I had not prayed. This does not mean that as the result of my prayers, my friend will necessarily be cured. Rather, as a result of my prayers, the God who enters my friend's life during his sickness, leading him to greater humanization through that sickness, is not exactly the same God as the one who would be entering his life if I had not prayed. In a real sense it is a richer God.

LIMITATIONS

Those who follow a more process-orientated spirituality must beware of reductionism. If it is possible to speak of God only in terms of this world, it is also true that one can only speak of this world completely in terms of God. And while it is true according to this model that the transcendent is a dimension of the secular,

[1] See Peter A. Campbell and Edwin M. McMahon, *Bio-Spirituality: Focussing as a Way to Grow*, (Loyola University Press, Chicago, 1985). The authors apply this less dualistic approach to spirituality. See for example pages 50 and following.

[2] This is, of course, very reminiscent of Teilhard de Chardin. Teilhard de Chardin's best known works are *The Divine Milieu*, (Collins, London, 1959) and *The Phenomenon of Man* (Collins, London, 1959). One of the best expositions of Teilhard's thought is that of Christopher Mooney, S.J., in his *Teilhard de Chardin and Mystery of Christ* (Harper and Row, New York: 1966).

or is the profane at its best and its most meaningful, it is still necessary to recognize this dimension explicitly. One cannot build a spiritual life based on a mere intellectual recognition that the sacred is the deepest aspect of the profane, and then act as if it is only the secular dimension which is of any significance. And while this model would be uncomfortable with clear-cut distinctions regarding the spiritual life, it is also true that growth takes place through clarification, and so at times it will be necessary to be clear, removing areas of ambiguity and blurring.

As is the case with the proclamation model, process spirituality can move in the direction of individualism. The individual may be viewed as isolated and self-sufficient, because perfection is seen as what is best possible for any one person. The notion of evil and sinfulness is not well developed in process thought and one can get the impression that history and human beings are self-redeemable. It is not always clear what the place of Christ is in this model. In that sense, the process model is unlike the mystery model in which the Easter-event is central. Again, while, like the sacramental model, it stresses the union which is based on relationality, it tends to be vague about the meaning of community. This may be due to the fact that it is so far removed from the institutional model.[1]

F. THE THERAPEUTIC MODEL[2]

DESCRIPTION

The incarnation shows us that God is most fully and clearly met in human interaction and experience. Our stories—our joys and sorrows, conversions and transformations—make sense only within the Christian story related in the liturgy. Human growth is consistent, even synonymous, with holiness and salvation. The primary image of the liturgy according to this model is Christian story-telling celebrated. This is the therapeutic model's particular expression of the root-metaphor of Christianity. The divine/human relationship is presented in parabolic fashion.

Of all the models, this one is the most phenomenological, in that it attempts to speak of divine reality in the language of ordinary human experience. It brackets metaphysical definitions about the liturgy. It does not demand an explicit philosophical framework on the part of the worshipper in order to speak of the worship of God. There may be an implicit one or several implicit ones but, to the degree possible, it prescinds from it. It is experiential, but not empirical. The liturgical scholar examines the high point of human living in order to find God there. The liturgy is a help in reading our history and the history of a community as a place where salvation is taking place. The presumption is that God is found in the humanization process and need not be introduced into it.[3]

This model stresses salvation in terms of humanization because it wishes to use more therapeutic images and concepts. The model is developed out of the

---

[1] *Worship: Exploring the Sacred.* See chapter five for a process-orientated approach to the liturgical community.

[2] *Ibid.* Chapter seven contains a fuller exposition of this liturgical model.

[3] This model has been developed from the insights taken from Gregory Baum's *Man Becoming,* (Herder and Herder, New York, 1970).

conviction that speaking about the worship of God through the articulation of the human clarification process is closer to the life of worshippers than through more metaphysical language. The model wishes to avoid being reductionistic in its use of more psychological categories. There are times in human life when we are led to greater self-knowledge, which enables us to triumph over past inhibiting patterns and seemingly present inevitabilities. These are not merely human. They are moments of salvation. The liturgy as well as our lives are more than meet the eye. Mere humanism is bad humanism.[1]

The need for this particular model of liturgy arises from the fact that people do not automatically or easily see how the salvational and humanization processes are inseparable. Many Christians refuse, or only reluctantly admit, that to become a better human being is to become holy. Holiness and psychological fragmentation in the same area of one's life is inconsistent. The liturgy can help the worshippers to see how a dysfunctional human life militates against personal and communal salvation. When we clarify under the assistance of God that there is something in us that inhibits as from wanting to know the truth and to recognize the evil in our lives and in society, we can speak of this clarification as being salvational. Worship is the way that the community assists in this clarification by giving support and direction to the worshipper.

Clearly, this model emphasizes the immanence of God. As in the process model, God is not imaged as being outside or alongside human history. In fact, according to this model, God is an object in no way. This is one of the most difficult aspects of this model to understand, especially since most liturgical texts presuppose an outsider God. This model prefers to treat God as *in* my knowledge and loving, rather than as the *object of* my knowing and loving. God is that dimension of human life which makes it impossible to reduce our humanity to mere humanity. But this dimension is not considered the object of a subject-object relationship nor the subject of a subject-subject (I-thou) relationship. American process theologian, John Cobb, has summed up this approach very well:

'I find God in the natural processes of my body, when these are not thwarted and impeded by external interferences. I find God in my feelings, when these are open and spontaneous. I find God in my reason, when this is drawn by truth rather than by the effort to justify myself. I find God in my imagination, when this is free and creative. I find God in my will, when it aims at justice and righteousness. I find God in my spirit, when it orients the whole of my life toward that which is worth achieving and frees me from petty self-serving concerns.'[2]

Since, according to this model, the presence of God is all-pervasive, God is certainly found in the liturgical assembly. It is the liturgical community which brings God out of concealment. For this reason the prayers are not understood as being directed to a God outside the assembly. This does not demand that all official liturgical texts be re-translated to fit this model, but rather that we attend to

---

[1] Some of these ideas are dependent upon the concept of self-transcendence as developed by Joseph Powers in his *Spirit and Sacrament,* (Seabury Press, New York, 1973). See especially pages 31 and following.

[2] 'To Pray or Not to Pray: A Confession,' in Maxie D. Dunnam (ed.), *Prayer in My Life,* (Parthenon Press, Nashville, 1974) p.97.

the fact that the context gives the meaning to the words used. The languages of the liturgy, the prayers, songs, and readings, are perceived as saying something about human salvation. And precisely because the liturgical texts find their best home in other models, such as the mystery and sacramental, this model demands that greater importance be given to the non-verbal. The breaking of the bread, the kiss of peace, bodily movements, and gestures often provide the milieu in which the texts themselves can be understood. Salvation itself is a bodily affair. Worship is the place where we can explore and experience God in a sensual, imaginative, and sexual way.

There is much about the process and therapeutic models which is similar. The process model, however, is philosophical, while the therapeutic is not. As in the process model, God is part of human history, but the therapeutic model emphasizes the transcendence of God in terms of critiques and new life in our personal and communal histories. Liturgy, therefore, celebrates the fact that all human life is under the critique of God. God is therapeutically present in the world.[1] God's transcendence is our transcendence insofar as, confronted by God, we deal with the destructive forces in our lives. The test of good liturgy is whether it leads to greater openness to truth and more availability to love.

The therapeutic model is hesitant to speak of God as a person outside the worshipper. When people are in touch with the deepest dimension of their lives, they are praying. God is more personal than a person. This hesitancy flows from the view that it is impossible to speak about God without speaking about oneself. It is a rejection of an objective or transcendent God as a theological starting point. Rather, story-telling becomes the way to approach theology. Story is the way that our lives are held together. Story allows us to transcend ourselves without moving beyond ourselves. Theology is an attempt to articulate the meaning of that story. In the liturgy, our own personal stories are incorporated into the larger story of Jesus Christ. Our story is a continual search for meaning and truth. The liturgy completes our own fragmented stories. When we enter into the Jesus story, we can re-interpret our own story of self-image. Salvation is the process of dealing with what needs healing in my life by re-interpreting myself, by telling my story in a different way. Often we need to be freed from an enervating, debilitating, life-story by discerning other possibilities. As one goes through the liturgical year, one's own story should take on many colours and dimensions. The clarification process which brings about redemption takes place through the story-telling. By celebrating the larger incorporating story of Jesus Christ, the liturgy becomes the place where Christian spirituality is experienced in a concrete way.[2]

As in the case of the proclamation model, the language of the liturgy needs to be evocative. It is not informational in character. It is rather the language of the parable which has a twist to it which challenges. And this language in the therapeutic model is the language of story. It is more explicit than the proclamation model in the call for shared vision and openness. The therapeutic model presupposes the incompleteness of life and the need to grow. The openness to reality which is called for is one which can see other possibilities in one's life. An

---

[1] This is a favourite expression of Gregory Baum.
[2] 'Storytelling and Christian Faith,' in *Chicago Studies* vol. 21:1 (Spring, 1982).

expanded sense of reality can bring about change. In therapeutic worship we as a community take into our personal histories the images of the celebrations throughout the year which stimulate our imaginations to entertain new ways of perceiving God. The clarification process of this model takes place by fantasizing and playing with a multiplicity of images. The liturgical assembly is the place where we can test various ways of looking at ourselves and our world. This makes it possible for the worshipping community to distance itself from its own way of seeing itself and the world, by playing with the story of the paschal mystery.

SPIRITUALITY
As is obvious from the above description of this model, therapeutic spirituality concretizes the Christian life in terms of human liberation and self-transcendence. God is not seen as calling us from a position outside ourselves. Spirituality is not simply equated with humanity, but what this model affirms is that there is something going on in the growth process of human beings which psychology cannot adequately explain.

Many who articulate their relationship with God according to humanization imagery will not be comfortable with much of the traditional language of the liturgy and prayer. Often the language they employ will resemble more that of the counsellor's office. And when they do use liturgical language, they will prescind from certain metaphysical commitments. The langauge of this form of spirituality will reveal more about the process of self-making, and respect for God will be translated into respect for others. What might be called self-analysis by the person with a different theological perspective, will be described as salvational by Christians who adopt this model.

This model of spirituality more than the others will call for bodily involvement. Salvation is celebrated by getting in touch with flesh and imagination. In this approach to spirituality bodily theology is not only a legitimate form of reflection on the faith, but is indispensable in our search for faithful understanding. For example, perfection in the model functions as a symbol. It is the same as the idea of wholeness. It is not some goal which is literally and finally to be reached. It is the kind of symbol which sets the direction for the traveller.[1] It is a call to constant movement in one's life. But it is not something to be reached concretely. It is to be oneself even though one may feel fragmented. But, in being oneself, one acts as if one's life pattern or story is related to a larger encompassing pattern. By my accepting all the elements of my life, both disruptive and dynamic, a sense of wholeness emerges.

LIMITATIONS
On the practical level there are some limitations to the therapeutic model. It is possible to become reductionistic and treat reality only within the psychological dimension. And often this can be employed to justify one's own inactivity or lack of direction. An obvious danger in the therapeutic model is the depreciation of the communal dimension of one's relationship with God. Since so much of the

---

[1] See Edward C. Whitmont, *The Symbolic Quest*, (Harper and Row, New York, 1969). p.135.

imagery is in terms of therapy, and since for so many this still has an individualistic character, this spirituality through humanization can be little more than
therapeutic growth formally baptized in the way that so much water baptism has
taken place: done without discrimination and without sufficient reference to the
praying church. And finally, while this model is promotive and supportive of the
Eastern styles of prayer in trying to avoid objectifying God, the dominance of
this model could be detrimental to the structured prayer of the church which
presumes, at least linguistically, that God is a person outside the worshippers'
growth life.

The therapeutic model needs the other liturgical models to complement what
it does so well, namely, connect one's internal history to one's liturgical life and
spirituality. But unlike the institutional model, it may de-emphasize one's
external history too much. In contrast to the mystery model, it might see the content of the liturgical rites solely in what the worshipper supplies. The possibilities
for an exaggerated individualism may need to be prevented through the
presence of the sacramental model.

In one sense the most serious limitation of this model is its attractiveness to
modern people. To speak of liturgy in terms of unconditional acceptance,
transparency, and empathy is very seductive, given the usual absence of these
qualities in present celebrations. How can one be against personal growth? In
the long run the test of the validity of the model is whether this personal growth
is redefined more deeply in terms of a responsible life in the church.

G. THE LIBERATION MODEL[1]
DESCRIPTION

The liturgy is the place where we experience in anticipation as well as rehearse
the establishment of the kingdom of God on earth.[2] It becomes the paradigm of
the breaking down of all human division and inequality. Our liturgy is offered
through Jesus Christ, the liberator, and all authentic worship must be contex-
tualized by reform of sinful structures and a ministry to the poor and oppressed.
The image of the liturgy according to the liberation model is the liturgy as
rehearsal of the kingdom, or as kingdom play. According to this model this
image is the best re-description of the root-metaphor of Christianity.

Obviously, this model of liturgical theology will view God, Christ, the
worshipping assembly, and the ritual actions from a liberation perspective. Both

---

[1] There are considerable similarities between this liturgical model and Dulles' servant
model of the church. Both stress the mission of the church to the world, that this mission is often to the suffering, poor, and oppressed, and that Christian 'praxis', the concrete living out of the historical dimensions of the faith, is the central imperative of the
gospel message. However, the servant model seems to centre around the image or
concept of diaconia, whereas the liberation model is organized around the image of
the kingdom. Both present a church which is active and dynamic in the world. They
convey an image of the church which is modern and relevant.

[2] For a good treatment of the place of the kingdom in liberation theology see John Topel,
S.J., *The Way to Peace* (Orbis Books, Maryknoll, 1979). See also Donald Senior, OP,
'The Reign of God' in *The New Dictionary of Theology*.

explicitly and implicitly, the liturgy will present a strong prophetic vision. Liturgy will be a place of witness: of those who wish to manifest their commitment to the poor and of the poor in turn bringing their own ministry to them. The scriptures will be read as validating statements of this contemporary witnessing. The liturgy will be planned in imaginative ways so that the liturgical assembly can be the place where Christians are called to be empathetic with the sufferings of others.[1] The liturgy is especially well equipped to do this, since this kind of experience is not easily brought about through exhortation and argumentation. The feelings and affective life must be 'convinced' if such empathy is to take place.

One of the most important ways in which the liberation model is made manifest in worship lies in how it acknowledges justice in the ministerial roles in the liturgy. They will be seen as epiphanies of the spirit rather than examples of power. The ritual structures themselves should break down distinctions of sex, age, race, class, or economy. Discrimination will have no place is this liturgy. The roles of ministry will be open to women and men, celibate and married. The language will be inclusive without bias toward the male gender when speaking of God as well as people.[2] Liturgical planning will be a team effort, inclusive of the presider. The team will be sensitive to where the community is in its prayer life. The best use of art will be in evidence. Variety and flexibility will characterize the planning. The environment of the liturgy must also be just.

The prophetic role of the liturgy calls for a response which promotes mutuality and an interchange of respect and trust. In the celebration the worshippers will find the challenge to go beyond their present life-styles and forms of commitment and service. This involves a conversion of life.[3] But it will usually be one which is more concerned with the rather pedestrian forms of injustice in ourselves and in our relationships. Liberation worship is for all at all times. It is not limited to those who are involved in apostolic activity or who find themselves in situations of great oppression. Establishing the kingdom of justice is not primarily a dramatic happening. It must also take the form of justice to oneself, that is, of self-acceptance and deep contact with one's bodily self. The liturgy can be a most appropriate place for the worker for justice to experience the justice in oneself, namely, that one is lovable and loved.

---

[1] *Worship: Exploring the Sacred,* see chapter eight, p.107ff.
[2] For a good treatment of liturgical language see Kathleen Hughes, *The Language of the Liturgy: Some Theoretical and Practical Implications,* (Washington, D.C., 1982-1985). (This occasional paper commissioned by ICEL is an excerpt from her dissertation: *The Opening Prayers of the Sacramentary: A Structural Study of the Prayers of the Easter Cycle).* For a detailed treatment of the matter of inclusive language see *Cleaning Up Sexist Language* (8th Day Center for Justice, 22 East Van Buren Street, Chicago, IL 60605, 1980). See also Mary Collins, OSB, *Worship: Renewal to Practice* (The Pastoral Press, Washington DC, 1987).
[3] Gustavo Gutteriez spoke of this in his foundational book, *A Theology of Liberation* (Orbis Books, Maryknoll, 1973) pp.204-5. One of his later books, *We Drink from our own Wells: The Spiritual Journey of a People* (Orbis Books, Maryknoll, 1984) has emphasized the spirituality of liberation.

Worship does not supply solutions for removing the injustice in society. It offers no recipes for how to deal with international conflict, debilitating family structures, or social tensions. The fact is that the kingdom of God will never be fully established. What the liberation model emphasizes is that the kingdom must be experienced in some concrete way *now*. It is not acceptable to wait forever in hope. It must be inaugurated in the present moment. And while the liturgy cannot tell us how this is to be, it can summon us to discernment about what may be our realistic approach to the issues of justice today. This discernment, however, must be communal. And it is worship which makes possible this process whereby the worshippers can get in touch with fundamental experiences of justice, or lack of them. From such insight they can move to action in building this kingdom.

In attempting to implement the liberation model of liturgy, one neuralgic point seems to be ever present. The question is: to what degree can politics and liturgy mix? What can be said to those who object to any political references in the prayers and preaching? The political life is so all-pervasive in human experience that to expurgate any references to it from the liturgy can only move worship to the margins of society, thus making it irrelevant.

Worship is so tied up with values that are significant for our daily living, that politics and worship must mutually interact. J. G. Davies sees this mutuality in a positive sense.

'Worship and politics are two ways of acting in God's world and they interpenetrate one another. Worship can provide guidelines for political action, while politics can put into effect that love which is at the center of the eucharist . . . worship can foster a vision of the kingdom of God, of human interrelatedness and then political involvement is needed to further the process of making that vision a reality.'[1]

This is one of the liturgical models in which an individualistic approach makes the least sense. The liturgical assembly is not gathered for itself, but for the world. When we assembly for worship, we acknowledge each other's presence. As worshippers we affirm our worth. Out of this affirmation can come the reconciliation with our brothers and sisters. And from this can emerge a commitment to change the values of an indifferent society. This is possible because liberation liturgy is found where we proclaim to others, both inside and outside the assembly, that we are called to move beyond self-interest and to be in communication with others. The saving message of Christ is effective in us when we identify with the poor and powerless.

As in the case of the therapeutic model, liberation liturgy also clarifies for us how the humanization process can be the salvific one. Human dignity and the unity of all peoples are the necessary conditions for salvation. As in the process model, there is no sacred/secular dichotomy. This is not to deny the worshippers' experiences of opposites: power/powerlessness, freedom/unfreedom, and oppressed/oppressor. The point is that such divisions can be transcended. By means of the liturgy as a place and form of communal discernment, the community and the individual can move to liberating freedom, power, and action.

---

[1] *New Perspectives on Worship Today*, (SCM Press, Ltd., London, 1978), pp.95-6.

The liberation model of liturgy has a liminal quality about it. Liminality here means the experience of transcending divisions of male and female, rich and poor, the person and the group, what is and what is not yet. Since the liminal experience is the challenging and removal of all status barriers, in this kind of liturgy the dispossessed come into possession, and the poor are made equal to the rich. Although powerless, the marginalized become powerful. This power celebrated in the liturgy is real because it is based on Christian hope and informs the worshippers' imaginations. But it is also clearly the 'anticipated power' of Christian eschatology.[1]

Injustice is omnipresent and overwhelming. How can one address it without losing hope? How can we be sure that we are not merely responding out of our personal agendas? It is the liberation liturgy which cuts through our egocentricity and self-hatred which we may project onto the oppressed. The liberation liturgy places the justice concerns in a commitment which is nourished by Christian hope.

A liberation model liturgy is ritualized contemplation in action. Contemplative action or active contemplation results in a revolutionary vision which brings about liberation. As I have written:

'The playful aspect of liturgy arises out of contemplation, the prophetic aspect out of action. The kind of contemplation referred to here is the listening to oneself and to others as powerful or powerless. It is shared reflection of the lived experience of power/powerlessness. It is the discernment which is necessary to avoid the overpoliticizing of the liturgy, the exaltation of the unexamined life, and the liberator becoming the oppressor. Contemplation means being in contact with the source of power ... the God within history, within community, within oneself.'[2]

Liturgy is meaningless contemplation, if it is not the place where we can respond to ourselves in new and freer ways. Here we should find the strength to empower others. It should be a passage from an other-worldly vision to a new consciousness, from a 'we cannot' to a 'we can do something about this situation.' The liberation and therapeutic models have in common the mobilizing of the imagination so that the worshippers can have the resources to break out of the ways in which they have been excessively inculturated in their societies.[3]

SPIRITUALITY

A liberation spirituality will be characterized by an ethics of responsibility. Although the dominant image, the building of the kingdom of God, is strongly eschatological, liberation spirituality is very much a this-worldly one. Persons motivated by this kind of spirituality are social in their relationship with God. They find it impossible to pray as individuals alone. Prayer is the way of bringing to mind the ways in which God is present in limited human organizations and structures. It is done in solidarity with one's brothers and sisters so that prayer, whether liturgical or not, is the making perceptible the covenant which the

---

[1] See Leonardo Boff, *Liberating Grace* (Orbis Books, Maryknoll, 1979), pp.156-7.
[2] *Worship: Exploring the Sacred,* p.111.
[3] Ibid., see chapter 15, 'Liberation and the Imagination in the Liturgy.'

person shares with humankind. Prayer always has a direction beyond oneself into the lives of others, whether it be in the Christian community or beyond it. Generally, it is a spirituality which is comfortable with biblical language and imagery, and, perhaps at times, with quite conventional religious language. However, it deals with such expressions by hermeneutically experiencing them as ways in which human oppression and dehumanization is being challenged by them.

There is a strong sense of personal commitment in liberation spirituality. The commitment is for change, for conversion, for newness of life, for a revision of society. Usually, the purpose of one's spiritual life is seen as the task of tearing away the network of evil which governs our lives so that a genuine union with God can take place. It is not a spirituality which expects to be conflict-free. Confrontation might well be the measuring rod of the authenticity of this spirituality. At its best, this spirituality understands justice to oneself to be an integral part of justice for the world. And while it will call for justice before peace, it will also demand love before justice.

The liturgy according to the liberation model will be one primarily of raised consciousness for the worshippers. The interchange among the members of the assembly will have the character of prophecy and the social dimension of human living will colour the personal aspects of Christian prayer. The mission of the church will be explicitly articulated in the rite itself. Any call for personal conversion must be seen as arising out of the concrete situation of the assembly. Becoming a better Christian means distancing oneself from the structures of evil and oppression which are part of daily existence. Such a spirituality makes it possible for the liturgy to become rehearsal time for the drama of the kingdom. Thus, the liturgy can be that analogous experience whereby assembly members can recognize the presence of the kingdom or the lack of it in their ordinary experience.[1]

LIMITATIONS

There are clear limitations to the liberation model of liturgical spirituality. The most obvius one is the avoidance of personal issues and growth in favour of strategy planning to bring about a better world. Everyone else's consciousness needs raising except one's own. God can be reduced to ideology; Christ to the image of the angry one who cleanses the temple with violence; the church to basic communities; and the liturgy to campaigning for freedom. Working against discrimination can become a form of class distinction: those enlightened and those not. The view of the kingdom is that it must be totally realized now.

When this becomes the dominant model of spirituality, it is often the aspect of love which has been suppressed. Justice and love are confused or the former replaces the latter. Violence is seen as the way of fulfilling the gospel injunction

---

[1] For an extensive treatment of the relationship between liturgy and social justice, see James L. Empereur, S.J., and Christopher Kiesling, O.P., *The Liturgy That Does Justice,* (Michael Glazier, Inc., Wilmington, 1988).

of Christian charity. In fact it often reflects people's inability to love themselves and so external activities against oppression become a substitute.

Another limitation of the dominance of this model is that people do not identify where struggles are really taking place. They seek to extricate various forms of injustice others are suffering and are willing to struggle for that, but do not recognize the struggles of their own existence. But one's own struggles must become the divining rod for those that exist outside oneself. There must be a resonance between one's own justice to oneself and the justice one is trying to bring to others. It is not enough simply to challenge, confront, and destroy the web of evil surrounding the marginalized. There must be something offered to replace it. Truly liberated people sense what that is.

The temptation that faces those who favour the liberation model will be to try to avoid the tension between living for others and self-development and growth. Love for humankind, compassion for the poor, sick and oppressed should be the fruits of liberation theology. But so should personal, mystical experiences. If the liturgy reinforces the identification of the Christian message with some existing or future social order, then the gospel is reduced to a political platform. That the worshippers are concerned with issues of justice, is no guarantee that a liturgy is an action of the Christian community.

Specific problems may develop from an over-emphasis on the liberation model. For those who find themselves in a situation of being oppressors, it might mean that they would consider worshipping itself sufficient to achieve justice. On the other hand, the liturgy could make them feel so guilty that they are overwhelmed and unable to move to concrete action. For the oppressed, there is the possibility that the liturgy could inject a sense of unreality in their lives, romanticizing their daily lives as better than they really are. Or the liturgy could so mobilize their angers that worship becomes the way of correcting societal wrongs. For both oppressor and oppressed, liturgy can become too pragmatic, too easily manipulable. Then there is no room for wonder, awe, fascination, and mystery.

3. Conclusion

Liturgical models for the most part are developed from models of the church which in turn are primarily dependent on scriptural and theological sources. This is especially true of the models presented here, with the possible exception of the process and therapeutic models. A problem with the more biblical models is that they tend to describe the liturgy as what it can and might be. The language can distract one from presenting conflict and problems that call for resolutions. Even a model of the church such as that of a community of disciples can easily be abstract and spiritualistic. For this reason, it is important to use liturgical models, all of them, together so that they can be mutually self-correcting.

It is important to bear in mind that liturgical models are theological. And for a credible liturgical theology these models need to be modified and grounded by the other two criteria: attention to the conclusions of the human sciences and the limitations of the praying church. As is the case with the other fields of theology, liturgical theology needs to be in serious dialogue with the social sciences. Such dialogue will bring a touch of realism to the more idealistic ways of imaging the liturgy. Adequate models of the liturgy of the contemporary church should be faithful to biblical and traditional sources but also must explore contemporary and social experience. There is no one model of the symbolic liturgy which can image for us how to worship in the future. In the face of sexual, racial, social, economic, and political oppressions as well as the possibility of nuclear holocaust, the liberation model will assume increasing importance with the continuing significance of the other models. But in the final analysis, all models work best when they are seen as inadequate. Liturgy still remains a mystery of faith.

Grove Liturgical Studies

This series began in March 1975, and has been published quarterly. Nos. 1, 3-6 and 10 are out of print. Asterisked numbers have been reprinted. Prices in 1987, £2.